SheFighter

From Trouble Maker to Global Change Maker

By Lina Khalifeh

SheFighter

By Lina Khalifeh

All rights reserved. This book contains material protected under International and Federal Copyright Laws and Treaties.

Any unauthorized reprint or use of this material is prohibited. No part of this book may be reproduced or transmitted in any form or by any means, electronic or mechanical, including photocopying, recording, or by any information storage and retrieval system without express written permission from the author.

© 2020 Lina Khalifeh

Cover designed by **RAMI KHALIFEH**
Cover Illustration by **AMANDINE DELCLOS**
Editor: **Art Fogartie**

Contents

DEDICATION	4
WHO'S WHO	5
ALONE IN AMMAN	6
A LIGHT IN THE DARKNESS	24
GETTING STARTED	32
THE TUNNEL	46
THE LONG ROAD BACK	50
SARA STARTS IT	58
BASEMENT BEGINNINGS	64
SHEFIGHTER	71
WHAT IT TAKES	85
CHANGING LIVES – ONE AT A TIME	90
HELPING THE HELPLESS	99
IT'S NOT ABOUT AWARDS	104
"DON'T PINCH ME – I MIGHT WAKE UP"	114
ACKNOWLEDGEMENTS	118
BIOGRAPHY	119

Dedication

I DEDICATE THIS BOOK TO:

My Taekwondo coach and mentor, Wa'el Al-Assaf, who always believed in me when I was training and competing in Taekwondo.

My mother, Majda Zidan, for her efforts to support my education and my passion for sports.

My father, Jalil Khalifeh, for training me to find solutions, he made me a fighter.

My grandmother, Fairouz Zidan. She ran a hair salon for thirty years. Her tip and savvy advice have always helped me. It makes me proud when she says I inherited her "powerful" nature.

Empowering Women Through Self-Defense

Who's Who

A list of the essential (and non-famous)

ALIA: A dear friend

JALIL: My father

JAMAL: a.k.a. "Big Bully"

LINA: Me

MASTER ALI: My first and best Taekwondo coach and teacher

MASTER OMAR: Owner of the dojo where I trained

MOE: My best childhood friend

MS. LAILA: A compassionate teacher

NIDAL: My brother

RASHA: My sister

REEM: My little sister

SARA: The woman who inspired me to start SheFighter

Empowering Women Through Self-Defense

Chapter 1

Alone In Amman

Nothing can dim the light that shines from within.
                                           Maya Angelou

My name is Lina Khalifeh and I am from Amman, Jordan.
Khalifeh is not a Jordanian family name – it is Palestinian, a fact destined to make a profound impact on my life. I hold a Jordanian passport; I am a citizen. But as I grew older, I realized the undying tribal nature of my home region. My grandfather was a refugee from Palestine who came to Jordan in 1948.

Seventy years later, our family is still does not quite belong. Assimilation in the Middle East does not happen in a few generations. We have been trying to make it work for generations – still do not have it right.

Father wanted to name me "Palestine." My life would have been a nightmare – traveling … going to school … breathing! My mother told him, "I will name the girls – you name the boys."

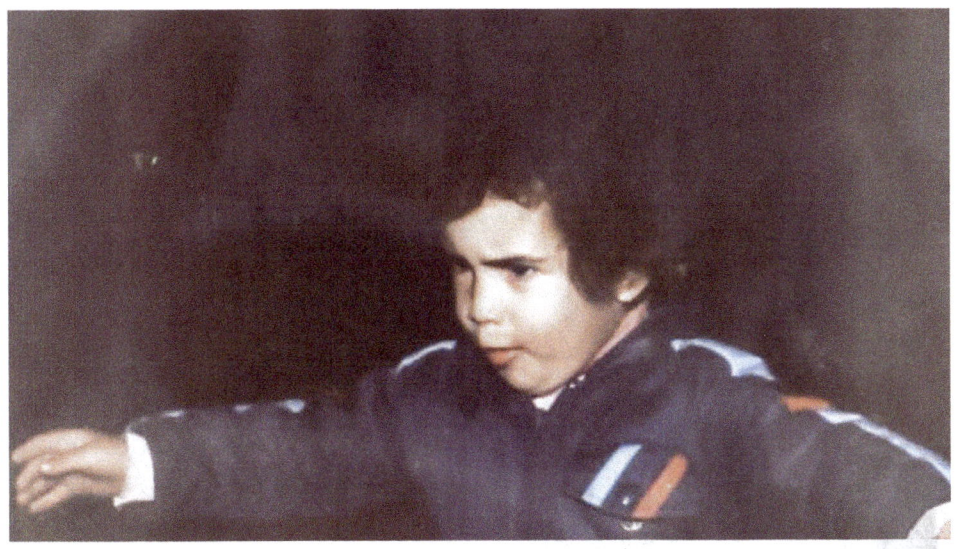

-Lina, age 3

I got "LINA" thank goodness

My brother is named Nidal – in Arabic it means, "Fighting against a system or country."

I am the second child in a family of four; I have an older brother and two younger sisters. Somewhere along the line, there was a mix-up – no one from the outside would ever suspect I belong to this group.

I have been "a tomboy" as long as I can remember. I kept my curly hair short, I dressed in boy's clothes, and all my friends were boys.

My mother, Majda, did not care. "It's a phase all girls have," she would tell my father who would "Hrumph" and return to whatever he was doing before he'd taken the time to disapprove of whatever I was doing. Once he grew concerned, it was too late.

I was a kid. What did I know about gender roles? And I certainly was never going to let anyone pick out my favorite color.

Pink? Seriously – pink?

-Lina, age **4**

Luckily, I grew finally comfortable in my own skin; I was who I was and I still am.

After school, girls stayed in the house and played with dolls – oh gross! I couldn't wait to get home after school every day, have lunch, change my clothes, and run into the streets to play football ("soccer" to Americans) in the street with the boys.

Only one problem – they didn't want me to play with them.

Two problems, actually. They did not want me to play with them and they beat me up every time I tried.

***

Big Bully was the worst. His name was Jamal. Whenever I saw him, I heard a voice in my head: Watch out for Big Bully. He loved to chase me, catch me, then beat me. No – it was not some demented form of puppy love. He was not trying to get my attention (though a left hook to the face certainly did) – he was not "showing affection the only way an immature boy knows how." No, he beat the stuffing out of me every day to drive home an engrained cultural understanding – girls belong inside.

Jamal gave me my first scar. He was chasing me, no doubt to hit me. I tripped and fell, face first, onto a broken bottle. My lip exploded in a scarlet eruption. There was blood everywhere.

Empowering Women Through Self-Defense

My mother's face radiated panic; she did not know what to do. She tried to staunch the flow with a wet towel – no use. We headed to the hospital where three doctors worked on my wound. Well, only one – the other two held me down while I wriggled, kicked, and screamed.

Six stitches later, I was well on my way to a scar – I continue to display it as a badge of honor. My lip was black and blue for two weeks; I could barely eat or drink. I took water from a spoon. It hurt so badly, I cried with every sip. Every time I opened my mouth, I learned a new definition of "pain."

Many people believe that sickness and injuries come as divine punishment. My culture promotes the thought; at the time, I thought I was being punished for playing with the Now I know the idea is nonsense, but I struggled with the guilt stemming from that incident for a long time.

At a very early age I learned that life is not fair – and the world is not always a happy place where balloons float lazily past the unicorns frolicking in the field. Life can be brutal – and unkind – and mean.
Everywhere in the world.
Especially to women.

Despite my scar – and the guilt – I insisted on being outside. I felt I belonged out there – staying inside was torture.

"Lina! You don't get it, do you? No – girls – on – the – team!"

Jamal accentuated every word with a punch or a slap or a kick. Either I did not care, or I wasn't too bright, because I was back the very next day, eager to join the game.

Every, single day.

"Are you deaf?" he asked. What are you doing here?"

"I just came to play." I answered.

"The streets don't belong to girls, go home!" he said.

"I don't want to go home. They may not belong to girls, but they belong to me"

He pushed me hard. "Are you not happy with your one scar? Leave, or I'll give you another one."

In a television movie someone would have stood up for me – most likely my brother. But, Nidal did not want to lose friends, and he certainly did not want a beating of his own. When Jamal said, "Get her," Nidal watched it happen.

One day – I don't know if I got there late or if I was wising up – I followed them from a safe distance. I hid behind bushes and other stuff while they made their way to the game site. I did not understand the prohibition. What was the big deal? The question never left my head.

I just wanted to play.

The ball rolled toward my hiding place. If I'd given the matter any thought at all, I would have stayed out of sight. But if I'd stayed out of sight – or if I'd given the matter any thought at all – I would not be Lina. I jumped up and kicked the ball as hard as I could. The ball took off like a rocket and landed ...

Empowering Women Through Self-Defense

…squarely between Jamal's eyes. His feet shot out from under him like he was on a sheet of ice (not a likely occurrence in Jordan, but you get the picture).

His face contorted in rage. "You are dead!"

I took off, safe in the belief they were neither fast enough nor smart enough to catch me. What I lacked in common sense, I more than made up for with self-confidence. Fortunately, I was right – at least that time.

I hid in a neighbor's backyard, standing behind a wall and holding my breath while I listened to the boys wondering where I had gone.

"No way she jumped that wall," Jamal said.

They agreed and left. I ran home.

Why did I have to run? And why was my heart beating so fast? I wasn't tired.

When I got home, I locked the door. My mom started asking questions.

"What's going on?"

"Nothing" I answered, breathing hard.

"Did you have fun?"

"Yes" I answered quickly and went to my room.

***

They bullied Moe, too. Moe was overweight, and the kids ridiculed him. Sometimes they would hold him down and stuff cake in his mouth until he cried. Moe always played goalie – he was too big to run after the ball. The kids kicked the ball as hard as they could, hoping to hit him in the face.

Moe was my best friend – a companion in the fellowship of suffering. "Stand up for yourself," I said.

"I can't," he said. "If I say anything, they will just beat me up. Lina, I am not you."

***

The next day, the boys on the bus glared at me with murderous intent. Mom waved goodbye.

My brother slid over. "You can't keep bothering us," he said. "Don't you get it? These are my friends. You don't belong outside with them. You should stay inside with the other girls."

I stared out the window.

"He'll hit you again if you come back," he said. "And I will not defend you."

"I know, because you are just like him," I answered.

"I warned you," he said. "You are on your own."

Big deal, I thought. I always have been.

Empowering Women Through Self-Defense

It's not easy being a kid and feeling like an outsider. I kept thinking about running away. I wasn't happy. I wanted my freedom to be outside all the time. None of the other girls liked what I liked – heck, they didn't like me. At school, I spent break times all alone, usually by choice. If you ask me, I cannot tell you what the girls were playing – I wanted to play with the boys.

The girls thought I was weird.

The boys thought I was weird.

Mother and Father thought I was weird.

Maybe they were right.

But I was me – that's all that mattered.

I never told Mother, but I cried in my room sometimes. Life in the "middle world" – straddling the chasm between boys and girls – and belonging to neither was tough and lonely.

I wanted to hit – something – someone. I wanted to start swinging and not stop until I was too dizzy to stand. Sometimes I lay on my bed and imagined escaping – I guess all children do. In my fantasies, I could fly. I soared all over the world, met famous people, and visited fabulous places. (Little did I know what life had in store.)

I tried to make an airplane once – from cardboard. I expected it would fly like a bird. Somewhere along the way, I forgot about the engine. The plane did not soar – surprise.

Making things fascinated me. I built a chair once – wooden. I was so very proud – until I sat on it and it collapsed. Turns out I am good at building things, just not aircraft and furniture.

Every so often, someone helped me. I went to an all-girls school. Little girls can be very cruel. One day, I left my desk to throw away some napkins. As I passed, I heard some girls on the front row. They were acting like they were whispering, but they knew I could hear.

"I don't know why her parents didn't name her Mohammed or Ahmad. She's such a boy."

"And her hair is so ugly."

"It looks like a tree."

"No, it looks like a bush. I bet she never combs it."

"She can't – she would lose the comb."

"Yes (giggles), then the bugs in there would have something to play with."

"It looks like falafel."

(The giggles turned to laughter.)

I turned. "You know I can hear you. My hair is better than yours and I like it. Stop bothering me."

Ms. Laila called to me.

"Lina, come here, please."

Ever dutiful and obedient, I hurried to the front – absolutely sure I had done something else wrong.

She kept her voice low, leaning in as she spoke. "Are those girls being mean to you?"

I didn't say anything.

"Lina." She did not raise her voice. Her tone was an odd mixture of intensity and compassion. "Tell me the truth – you know you are always supposed to tell the truth. Are they being mean to you?'

I nodded.

"Tell me," she said.

How no one in the room heard me gulp, I do not know – the swallow sounded like someone beating on a trash can with a hammer.

"They…they said my hair is too curly and ugly like a tree – and it looks dirty. They said it looks like Velcro because everything sticks to it."

"They are being mean because you are different from them – and you frighten them."

That made no sense to me – none at all.

"Why?"

"Because you will not change just so you can be in their group. You know what you want and You need to stand up for yourself. They are afraid of you because you are not afraid at all."

I stood there not knowing what to say.

"Did what they said about your hair hurt your feelings?"

"No," I said.

"You have great confidence, Lina. You are strong. You know who you are. I am proud of you,

I smiled at her and went back to my desk. I didn't care what they thought of me.

Still, when I stared out the window at night – when sleep avoided me just like the girls at school, I sometimes asked, "Why can't I just be like everyone else?"

***

Math bullied me, too. It did not come to me naturally, so I struggled. Today, I might be diagnosed with ADHD or something like that, but what I remember was that whenever I was in Math, I was bored.

My math teacher loved to read grades aloud. She called the name, "Amal," and the mark, "97," and Amal or Jasmine or whomever would strut to the front of the class and accept the paper like they were receiving a land grant from the King Hussein. Some of them held the trophy over their head – a world championship belt.

Geez, it's just a stupid paper.

But I always knew what was coming.

"Lina" … and then a grade that usually began with a "forty … fifty … or (if I'd had a particularly productive round of guessing) … a sixty." It was the most humiliating experience of my young life.

Until…

We were in Math class and it was time for the Ritual of Embarrassment – also known as the announcing of the weekly mathematics marks.

"Samah … 85." Samah acted like she'd won the lottery. She was usually my only hope of not being the worst grade. Things were looking up – if she had managed an 85, maybe I did well.

"Hala … 100."

A surprise to no one – the Laws of Nature: the sun rises in the east…what goes up must come down…Hala makes a perfect score on a math quiz

Several other names – nothing remarkable. Then, dread seized my heart. Suddenly, I knew – I don't know how, I just knew – I had done poorly. My grade was always miserable…always among the lowest. Anxiety screwed its way into my throat … then into my stomach … then into my bladder.

I peed myself.

Simultaneously I felt the warm wetness and heard my name. "Lina, you got four of twenty. That is the lowest grade in the class – one of the lowest I have ever seen. Either you are not trying, or you are stupid – I don't know which, but you should be ashamed of yourself." I was, but for a reason not at all related to my miserable performance in class.

Eight years old … I was eight years old. And I was squishing at my seat.

"Lina, come get your paper. Honestly, if you keep this up, you will be in this class next year and all your friends will be in the next grade."

Riveted to my seat, I heard the other children beginning to giggle. Several of them pointed – not at me, but to the puddle on the floor in front of my chair.

"Lina!"

I slid from my place and walked forward, praying that, somehow, the dark spot on the front of my school uniform would miraculously disappear. It didn't.

The class howled.

The teacher shook her head. "Go to the toilette," she said. She waved her hand like she was shooing away a bothersome fly.

I went to the toilette. There was no toilette paper to use and I started crying. My mark was bad. I was worried about what mother and father would say. I was very embarrassed.

Two girls from tenth grade passed by the toilette and saw me crying. "What's wrong?"

I stopped sniffling long enough to answer. "I need toilette paper and I don't have any."

They found some. When they gave it to me, one of them said, "Don't cry. You're too cute to cry."

I felt better. All though my life, I have felt that no matter how difficult the situation, God would send an angel to help me and to remind me, "You are okay, Lina. Keep going."

That thought helped build a warrior.

When Mother picked me up – they called her from the Office, at least I got to go home early – she was furious. "Why didn't you excuse yourself?" she asked.
I did not bother to explain.

After school, I headed outside in search of the soccer game. Jamal was there.

"I remember what you did," he said. "You kicked the ball at me on purpose."

"And you fell over like you were dead," I said. I might not have been very bright in Math, but I was fearless.

I never saw the rock, but I felt it smash into the side of my face, right next to my eye. Mother must have been watching from the window because she was out of the front door as I crumpled in a heap.

Jamal ran – coward.

I expected nursing and sympathy. I got nursing and a lecture.

"How many times did I tell you to stop going outside, Lina? I will talk to his mother about this, he can't just throw stones at other kids like this! Still, you keep goading the boys. You should not go out there. Why can't you play dolls inside with the other girls?"

I knew Mom was talking but I didn't do anything but cry.

Mother kept me home from school the next day and kept a bag of ice on my eye. Once everyone came home, I sat at the window and watched the boys playing football. When I went back to school, I could barely see. The left side of my face was a bizarre rainbow of yellow, blue, black, and purple – maybe even a little green. I was the talk of the school.

The letters blurred – the pages swam. It didn't matter. I hurt too much on the inside to care.

Life disintegrated into a sticky miasma of agony and loneliness. I knew I was ugly. I knew my hair was hideous. I knew I looked and acted like a boy. I didn't know how to communicate with girls, with boys, with teachers, with my parents, with my siblings – with anyone.

School was a continual struggle. Because of its reputation for excellence in teaching English and French, we attended a Roman Catholic School. My family is Muslim. Maybe the teachers went out of their way to be tough on the Muslim students – maybe past events were more trying in my mind than in reality. But I vividly remember that Muslim teachers (all female) were banned from wearing their hijabs.

The Principal was well-known for her punishment techniques. If any girl was performing badly, the Principal would call her to the front of the 8 AM assembly and slap her in front of everyone. Teachers and administrators checked attire. Each sock was to be 5cm below the knee. The Principal carried a big stick. If the socks were not right, the offending student was asked to step to the side, then popped on the legs with the stick until the tears flowed.

The nuns were horrible to us. When we walked to class, they would accost us and make us kneel. Then they hit us on the back with their sticks. Why was I kneeling in front of a human being? They were not God.

I am not a Christian, but I am pretty sure what they did is not part of the Christian tradition – kneeling before another person.

Father wanted us in public schools, they were cheaper. But Mother was the driving force behind our education and she would not accept the substandard nature of the public situation. Additionally, public school teachers were allowed to administer corporal punishment. Mother would not tolerate anyone beating her children.

Since my parents were liberal (we were never forced to cover our heads), they did not object to the treatment we received in school, but there was a none-too-subtle sense in the school that the Muslim students were "less than."

One day, the teacher assigned the "multiplication tables."

"You have until tomorrow to learn them," she said. "If you do not know them, there will be terrible consequences."

I was a brave girl, but not in school. I think I cried all night. It's hard to learn 7x8 through a wall of tears.

The next day was awful. The teacher walked between the rows of desks, randomly selecting students.

"What is 12x11," she asked.

When the student gave a correct answer, the teacher nodded, and the student sat."

"Lina."

I stood.

"What is 6x3?"

"18."

She asked another. "What is 5X7?"

"35."

Another. "What is 9x6?"

"54." I was sure I was in the clear.

"Lina, what is 9x8?"

I hesitated – two beats too long.

"Hold out your hands," she said.

I did. She thwacked my open palms four times each with a thick wooden stick Well, not exactly. She got past my right hand fine, but on the third strike to my left hand, she hit me so hard, the stick broke.

She looked at me.

"Aren't you going to cry?' she asked.

I shook my head.

"Why not?"

"It did not hurt," I said. It was a lie, but I was not going to give anyone the satisfaction of making me cry – ever again.

She threw me out of class.

When Mother heard the story, she was livid. The next day, she came to the school and "discussed" the situation with the teacher. When the teacher returned to the class, her cheeks were red.

"Lina," she said. "Come to the front."

I went.

She slapped my face – hard. Her hand was immense. My face was small. The humiliation stung more than the blow, and the slap almost dislocated my jaw.

I kept my head down, too embarrassed to look at anyone.

"I feel better," she said.

I did not cry.

As soon as Mother heard the story, she withdrew us and enrolled us in a different school. (The Government banned beatings in school in 2009/2008 after a video of a teacher punishing a student went viral.)

Mother still gave me speeches about playing with the boys – about staying inside with the girls, but I did not need them anymore. Very soon, I found something else – I found a place to belong – I found a place to dominate.

Chapter 2

A Light in the Darkness

Your children are not your children. They are the sons and daughters of life's longing for itself. They come through you but not from you, and though they are with you, yet they belong not to you.

Kahlil Gibran

"We should sign the children up – all three of them."

Mom was excited. It was early. I rubbed the sleep from my eyes and tried to focus.

"A new Taekwondo school is opening close by in a few days. I don't like them on the streets all day. Besides, Taekwondo will be good for them."

Taekwondo? I thought. Seriously?

Middle Eastern girls do not usually train in martial arts – at least not in my generation. My ears burned … my fingers tingled … my heart pounded.

Taekwondo! I liked the sound of that. I could see my father's head nod in disinterested approval.

On the last day of school, the final five minutes lasted for hours. When the bell finally sounded, I raced to the car.

"Let's go!"

Mother looked at me with an eye roll. "We have to wait for your sister. Take it easy."

Rasha's enthusiasm level was a tad lower than mine. When she crawled into the car – a condemned woman headed to the executioner – she started whining. "I don't want to go. I don't like Taekwondo."

Mother shook her head. "How do you know? You have not tried it. You might like it."

Sister scowled. "No, I won't. Why do I have to do this?" I feared her lack of cooperation might screw up my chances.

Before she could offer every child's favorite line, It's not faaaaaaaaair," I said, "Let's go. Let's go," as if I could combat my sister's petulance with chatter.

"Relax, Lina," Mother said. "We are going."

When we arrived at the dojo, I heard kids screaming – Aice – Aiceeee! I could smell the sweat of burning muscles. The walls reverberated with the thump of bare feet against leather targets. I saw students (boys and girls) in white gis pulled together at the waist with belts of varying colors. A palpable energy surged through the air – and into me.

"Hello."

I turned to meet Master Ali. "Welcome to our school. I will be your teacher. I will take very good care of you." He shook my mother's hand, then looked at me. "I can tell you are ready to pursue your black belt. You want to start competing against the other girls."

"Yes," I said – though I am sure I shouted. " I am very excited."

He bobbed his head. Then, again to Mother, "Shall we try on some uniforms?"

Gi in hand, I raced to the locker room. My hands trembled as I pulled on the tunic. I smiled at white-belted image in the mirror.

The second my bare feet touched the Taekwondo mat, I felt a power I had never know before – ever.

The Master showed us how to bow to the class – and to him. And it began.

Rasha and Nidal did not like any of it. They quit within a month. I kept training three times a week. The mats became as essential to my life as oxygen. On the mats, I was home – on the mats, I was whole.

The transformation was outstanding. My math teacher had called me "stupid" – I was constantly ridiculed by my peers because they thought I could not do anything right. But, at Taekwondo, before too long, the Master was saying, "You students, watch the way Lina does this."

I was good – I was very good.
"Lina is never late – Lina trains hard – Lina respects the discipline."

No one had ever told anyone to "be like Lina."

One afternoon, after I had been in training for two years Mother came to fetch me. Master Ali took her aside.

"Lina has the heart of a fighter – a warrior. She has been training very hard. She needs to go to the next level."

Empowering Women Through Self-Defense

"What is that?" Mother asked, anticipating the need to bring me to more classes, more often.

"She needs to compete on a wider scale. She needs to enter tournaments."

More anxious than excited, Mother said, "Won't she get hurt?"

Master Ali nodded slightly. "She will get banged up some. Bruises are inevitable. It is combat, after all. But I do not anticipate anything major."

I was surprised by My mother's response. "Okay," she said. On the way home, she turned to look at me. "We are willing for you to do this, but only if you promise to be diligent in your school work."

I would have promised to eat glass at that moment.

***

I was Eleven at that time. I fell in love with Taekwondo from the moment I first stepped onto a mat. Something about the structure, the intensity, the focus, resonated with me. It was as if I could hear a voice saying, "This is where you belong."

Some kids sit down at a piano and can play almost immediately. Turn on the television almost any night and you will see a three-foot tall boy who sings like Bruno Mars (well, almost). Children can learn to do outstanding things at very early ages.

I was like a little duckling – and Taekwondo was a luxurious pond in which I wanted to paddle as long as anyone would let me. In the sports world, I was a "natural." The moves came easily. I was fluid, almost from the very beginning.

After the first day, all I wanted to do was learn and train. I wanted to perfect a move, retain it, and learn another. I stopped my quest to play with the boys. In fact, one day Jamal asked my brother, "Where is your sister?"

Apparently, Jamal was bored because he didn't have anyone to hit. I guess I put Big Bully out of business. (To complete the story, we eventually moved to a different neighborhood. I never saw Jamal again.)

But school remained a challenge. Don't ever let anyone tell you girls do not bully. Girls can be vicious. I was 14 years old and in ninth grade. Everyone knew I was in martial arts class. But Taekwondo was "for boys" and my classmates never let me forget it. Break times and lunch were tough because I was still usually alone. No one wanted any contact with the strange girl who did martial arts.

Except for one – one particularly memorable day.

Aisha loved to hear herself talk – and she always wanted everyone to listen. She swaggered through the school with a flock of little minions who laughed at all her jokes and told her she was great. Aisha was just another in a long line of bullies. One day she decided to get her followers to teach me a lesson between class breaks. Suddenly, four girls grabbed me. They held my arms. Aisha started punching me in the stomach. I took it for about three seconds.

Then …

… Aisha's glasses broke into four pieces when my kick found her face. Her "brave" friends immediately let me go, but they kept me from giving Aisha the pummeling she deserved.

The School's administration determined the encounter was my fault. After all, I was the girl who would not act like one. They locked me in a room from 10:00 AM to 2:00 PM – no food – no contact. No one bothered to listen to me. No one did the five-against-one math.

It must have been my fault. After all, I was different.

Therefore, I was the perpetrator.

The bullies were not punished.

Mother said, "Always know this, if someone lays his hand on you, you beat them up and defend yourself, I will not always be there to defend you, you need to learn how to stand strong for yourself." Father said, "We don't want any trouble. Don't do anything."

The next morning, some of the girls stayed home. Their parents called the school. "Lina is going to attack our daughters."

I was suspended for three days. Before I was readmitted, I had to sign a document promising not to hit or harm anyone.

There were a few friends – older girls who either were not threatened by my lack of femininity or who did not care. We played volleyball occasionally. But as far as my own peer group, I was alone – isolated – and ridiculed.

"God will curse any girl who looks or acts like a boy," they said. "You are upsetting God because you will not accept your role as a woman. He will not take care of you when you grow up."

My friends pressured me to buy feminine clothes and to act more like a woman. But I stayed true to myself.

I was content to be "the girl with muscles like a boy."

***

Training intensified – I was going every day. Mother grew weary of bringing me after school. Pretty soon, I was riding a bus.

I began to dream of Olympic competition, fighting and beating the best in the world – coming home with a cluster of gold medals draped around my neck. Having friends at school no longer mattered. Master Ali was my best friend – he believed in me and in my quest.

I raced for the bus every day after lunch. Master Ali was right – I got bruised. But I loved every one of them – they were my badges of honor and hard work.

I stayed at it. I trained like a maniac. Finally, Master Ali said, "Do you think you are ready?"

In my mind, I could see Jamal. All I said was, "I was born ready."

Ha!

Flying Turning Kick

Chapter 3

Getting Started

*You are not a drop in the ocean,
you are the entire ocean in a drop.*

Rumi

"What happened?" I could hear my voice – and feel the throbbing in my head.

"Your opponent landed a backside kick in your stomach. You could not breathe. You dropped like a full can of paint," the Master said.

Despair flooded my heart. "I am terrible," I said. "I can't beat anyone outside of the dojo."

Master Ali placed his hand on my shoulder. "Lina," he said. "You are a blue belt. Your opponent has a black belt. She has been doing this longer. She is simply better than you at this time. But she will not be better than you forever. Everyone loses at first. There is no disgrace in losing. There is only disgrace in accepting defeat as a way of life."

He was right. He knew I should not have been in the fight – I was overmatched. But he wanted me to get my feet wet – and my rear end kicked!

The defeat pushed me. I trained every single day. When the sessions ended, I jumped rope until I reached 3000 repetitions – every day. I hung a punching bag in my room and worked out after I finished school assignments. My parents did not love the constant thump and whack, but they lived with it. At least I was not trying to play football with the boys. Many days I ran before I left for school.

I endured catcalls and honking cars. Women in Jordan were not "into" physical fitness – I was the only female on the street in jogging attire.

Just after my fifteenth birthday, I earned my black belt. A time of trial – a test of character and will.

My father got the results and sent a message to the school.

The teacher called me to the front.

"Lina, your father sent you a message."

I was worried.

"He said to tell you that you were now a black belt – whatever that means."

With tears in my eyes, I returned to my seat. The members of my class applauded – all except Aisha. She glared.

The Chinese character (段 – used in the Korean language) for "dan," is translated as "step" or "stage." After black belt, students can add "dans" – an extra award or level. Each dan requires a test. I was determined to earn three dans – to become a master in Taekwondo. When I completed my first one, I placed second among the forty men and women who tested.

I took my second dan test and placed second among fifty men and women.

On the day before my third dan test, the Head of the National Team approached. His voice was loud – like a drill sergeant yelling at new recruits.

"Khalifeh!"

"Yes," I answered getting to my feet.

"You are Palestinian?" he asked.

"I am Jordanian," I said. "My family has lived here over fifty years."

"If I were you," he said, "I would not take the test tomorrow. You will not pass." Everyone stared. They'd never heard anyone speak like this before.

I was a little slow to catch on. "I'll pass," I said. "In fact, I am hoping to be in first place when it is over."

He shook his head. "You will not pass. I will see to it."

He might have been devious, but he was not stealthy. He made his threat – his promise – in front of at least twenty people.

I turned to Master Ali.

"Take the test," he said. "It will be fine."

It was not. During the test, I knocked down the man who was my opponent. I used my famous flying back side kick. Everyone thought I would place first.

I failed.

Taekwondo had instilled new self-confidence in me – and a strict sense of honor. If I had failed because I did not know the material – if I had failed from laziness or sloppy execution – I would have accepted my fate. But this was corruption in its basest form.

Empowering Women Through Self-Defense

I reported the incident to the Olympic Committee in Jordan – and I had corroboration from the witnesses. I was instructed to take the test again.

I finished second and received my third dan.

It was time to get back to fighting.

***

I joined the Taekwondo National Federation and began national competitions. Corrupt oozed out of every little crevice in the organization.

Instead of merit, the system relied on favoritism and influence. Knowing what I know now, my time with the Federation was wasted – an exercise in futility. But as the saying goes, "That which does not kill us makes us stronger."

Once a fighter is over 18, all bouts are by weight categories. Competitors must "make weight." If you are slotted for the 59 to 63 kilo class, you cannot have a single extra gram over 63 kilos. The Federation positioned the fighters. I normally competed in the 59 to 63k group. The Federation already had someone they liked in that spot. It did not matter that I could beat her – easily.

I won every fight in the 63-59Kg class.

"Lina, you will fight in the 58-55 class. I was always comfortable with my weight – I was (am still am) very muscular.

Taekwondo promotes long, lean muscles. Since muscle weighs more than fat, even at 62 kilos, I looked slender. I liked the way I looked and felt. When I fought at 62 k, I always won the gold.

I was fit. I was quick. I was strong.

Obviously, to qualify for competition in the 58-55 class, I had to lose weight. And I had to keep it off.

Sometimes, I went for an entire week eating only three dates and drinking water. When the fights came, I had no energy – I had not consumed any protein or carbs. How in the world was I supposed to fight? (The girls were allowed to go home with instructions to "Watch what you eat." The boys were required to stay in the dojo where people could monitor food consumption.)

I looked like a cadaver … pallid skin … poor complexion … sunken eyes.

Still, I was there to fight.

I remained in the 55 to 58 class for a year and I lost a lot. Certainly, I did not eat enough to maintain my strength. But there was a more compelling reason for my lack of success lay lurking in the hierarchy. The coach for one of the women in the 58-55 class – one of my competitors – also managed the referees.

During one fight, I could not score. No how often I landed a kick or a punch, I got zip! During a break, Master Ali told me, "Lina, you will not win unless you knock her down."

I put her on her back repeatedly. The referee never counted.

Her corner screamed, "Get up! Get up!" She stood and the match continued. I looked at the referee. No points.

I guess he'd never seen anyone fall down voluntarily so often. My situation was hopeless.

But I could not sustain the weight – I had too much muscle. I trained too hard. (Today, I am very comfortable at 60 kilos – my perfect weight.)

I had a signature move – a favorite – the Twi-myo Dwi Chagi (Flying Back Side Kick). Usually, I could knock down anyone in the first two minutes of a fight. I had very strong arms. When I punched an opponent in the chest, sometimes she had to quit because she could not breathe or because she had fallen and could not stand.

Once, Master Ali approached me. He was chuckling to himself.

"What's so funny?"

"You might not have anyone to fight," he said.

I could sense the Federation's slimy hand at work.

"Have I been disqualified or something?" I asked.

Master Ali shook his head. "No, everything is fine," he said. "I was just at the registration table. As soon as I put your name in at the 58k level, three girls withdrew theirs. They are afraid of you."

> But one girl was not afraid.

***

Coach Ali's voice was calm, but I could tell he was worried. "Lina, she is the gold medal champion of Asia," he said.

I looked across the mat. My opponent looked like a muscular giraffe!

"How tall is she?"

"One hundred-and-eighty-five centimeters; equivalent to 72 inches," he said.

I was 168 cm. At 6'5", I was six inches shorter. While we were in the same weight class, I was giving up a lot of reach.

She was strong – I was smart. My kicks landed like bee stings. The more points I took, the angrier she grew. No one – no one – had ever outpointed her. She started flailing and shouting.

Someone else was assigned to my corner during the competition. Coach Omar. I knew him – had known him for some time. He owned the dojo where Ali trained me. But there were things about Omar that I did not know – things I would discover – things that would change my future.

At the break Coach Omar said, "Don't keep doing the same thing."

"Why not," I said. "I am winning."

"Stop taking points. I am your coach for this match – fight the way I tell you. You will protect your lead and not take any chances."

I wanted Master Ali back in my corner, but I was powerless.

"I will fight my fight," I said. "I can beat her."

Master Omar flew into a rage. He'd been seated on a small camp chair. He picked it up and threw it at me. Imagine, any coach throwing a chair at any player. Still, no one moved to interfere.

I stared at this crazy man. "Fine," I said. "I'll do it your way."

I had won the first two rounds and was ahead three points. If we fought to a draw in the third round or if Goliath did not knock me out or out-point me severely, I would win.

She started taking points like I was giving them away. Point after point – kick after kick. The ending was inevitable – until I decided to change it.

I landed a few solid kicks and punches, tallied a few points and won the match 10-13. Everyone was thrilled – well, not quite everyone. I jumped around, happy that I won; the audience was silent. No one had expected me to win. The only people cheering for me were my mother and Master Ali.

I knew Master Omar would be angry, but my opponent's reaction stunned me. Martial arts are based on tradition and honor. You do battle with your opponent, the match is decided, and you give your respect , regardless of the outcome. There are hundreds – thousands – of years of tradition involved.

So, I was a little surprised when, as the referee held up my hand in victory, Lady Mount Everest punched me in the eye. Even though she was penalized, the match was already over – and no one could un-scratch my cornea.

Instead of defending me against such an egregious violation of behavior, Master Omar went nuts on me. "You never listen. You are a terrible fighter. I told you..."

I walked away. Something was not right. Any sane coach would be thrilled to have his (or her) fighter win any match – especially one against such an illustrious opponent. I found out the reason later.

As I said, Master Omar was the owner of the dojo. He had future plans for my opponent – plans to woo the undefeated champion onto our national team – a great coup and a significant marketing triumph. My pesky little kicks shattered his dreams.

I had just gotten another taste of the corruption of the Federation.

Things never really improved. The system was broken – rotting from the inside. Prince Hassan was in charge of Jordan's Taekwondo Federation. Every time he heard whispers (or shouts) about corruption, he fired everyone but when the next election was held, the same names – the same families – rose to the top of the leaderboard.

I've always thought it was like the mythical Hydra. When you cut off one of the snake's heads, two grew back in its place. Eradication of the corruption was never going to happen – at least not in time to help me.

***

This story has nothing to do with Taekwondo, but it says something about the culture in which I was Raised.

For reasons I have never known, Master Omar was running for the Jordanian Parliament. He was from a "big time" Jordanian family. He solicited my vote.

Not exactly.

"Lina, may I see your ID?"

I figured he needed it for a tournament or travel or something. I handed it to him.

"You get it back after you vote for me," he said.

I voted. He returned my ID.

He lost.

He ran again – and tried the old, "Let me see your ID" routine. I refused.

"I will vote for whomever I choose," I said. "And it will not be you."

Might have been brave – might have been the right thing to do – but it was not very helpful to my career. Later, I figured things out.

But God had to help me.

***

Soon, I had collected my twentieth gold medal. I was the best fighter in my weight class (63-59 kgs) in Jordan. Despite our differences, any time his dojo fought another one, Master Ali had me on the mats. The more I competed, the better I got.

Mother attended the competitions – and drove me for treatment.

When Father came home, he always asked, "Which hospital this time?"

My response never varied. "I won the gold medal, Father."

"You should quit someday. Taekwondo is not for girls."

At night, I lay in bed, grimacing occasionally when I rolled onto a bruise, but smiling as visions of Olympic victory flooded my mind.

When I was seventeen, I started international competition, a very big deal. (You should know that Jordan won its first Olympic gold medal at the 2016 Rio Olympics. Interest in the sport is now at a fever pitch. The wave was beginning to build as I was competing.)

I knew I would represent Jordan in the next Games. This was going to be a snap. I was a multiple gold medal winner – I knew I would qualify for matches. I had beaten everyone in the room on multiple occasions. All I had to do was train hard and the victories would continue.

But you cannot win if you never compete. And my chances to compete melted the second anyone on the Selection Committee said, Khalifeh. Were there nods? Knowing winks? Shaking heads? I am not sure – but there was no question about my heritage. In their quiet meetings away from prying eyes, I have no doubt someone always said: This is the Palestinian. Maybe they didn't, but the results spoke volumes.

Power, prestige, and position determined who went to the Competitions. The issue was not "how good are you," but, who are your people."

Harassment abounded – little men with power trying to assert control over women. I never tolerated it – not one touch – not one suggestive remark. I refused to flirt. I would not laugh at their slimy comments or inappropriate jokes.

Some of the girls went along. Some of the mothers bribed coaches with food and laughed like fools when coaches said things for which they should have been slapped. I did not want to play – I did not want anyone putting his hands on me. Everyone knew it.

And they did not like it. I guess I was supposed to "go along to get along."

So, I was not chosen to fight.

Disillusionment settled into my heart.

***

"Hold the target higher," I said.

Lama was not paying attention. I needed her to raise the leather kicking bag.

"Hold the target higher," I said again.

The coach's voice sliced the air like a malicious scythe. "Lina, do not talk during training."

Empowering Women Through Self-Defense

I did not bother with a response. He knew what I needed – there is no way he had not heard my request to my partner. Like all the other Federation coaches, he was just hassling the Palestinian.

I motioned with my hand for Lama to elevate the target.

"Lina," the coach's mouth was five inches from my right ear. "Drop and give me fifty pushups."

I delivered a vicious spinning kick, then motioned Lama to move the target even higher. I imagined the coach's head at the top of the leather bag.

"I said Give me fifty!"

When I whirled, he flinched as if afraid I would strike him. The thought never crossed my mind. I did not respect the man – or any of the coaches – but I always showed respect – always.

My voice was level and calm. "I was only asking for a higher target," I said.

He sneered. "Fifty." He pointed to the floor – a master ordering a dog to sit.

I turned back to Lama and unloaded a vicious rising kick.

Again, I signaled for an even tougher mark. Now, he was shouting.

"Lina, I order you to give me fifty pushups. If you do not, you are off the team."

I did not say anything. I just stared at the wall just over the coach's shoulder. The dojo fell deathly quiet. I saw red beginning to tinge the coach's ears. He was angry, and he was determined to humiliate me. His voice echoed off the walls at full volume.

"I said *fifty*!"

Something snapped.

"You cannot kick me off the team," I said with more confidence than I felt. "I quit!"

I gathered my bag and walked out of the gym.

I never went back.

Chapter 4

The Tunnel

I felt like a lion with a chain around its neck, not degraded by the chain, and not complaining, but just waiting for my powers to be recognized.

Rumi

Master Ali took me back. He was pleased I had left the National Team.

"They are corrupt and foolish. It is their loss" he said. "Don't worry about it."

If he knew – and I am sure he did – the prevailing reason for my lack of acceptance, he never mentioned it. He worked for Coach Omar – a pure Jordanian. Master Ali remains a courageous man – but he is not a fool.

Then he nodded, and we went back to training.

Master Ali is a man with a quiet personality. While a man of great internal fortitude, he had no political power – he carried no clout. He grew up in great poverty. His mother abandoned him. When he was still young, his father and brother died in the same month – he had no one.

He had only Omar – who paid his salary and treated him like a member of his own family.

If you are expecting a happy ending, you will be disappointed. Nothing ever goes as smoothly as I would hope.

You see, Ali was fine with my decision. But Omar was not.

Omar peered at me like I was something unpleasant on the bottom of his shoe. "Who are you to question the Federation?" he asked. "You are just a fighter. The Federation is made up of the greatest leaders in this sport in the entire country. Go back, apologize, and resume your training."

I did not move.

"Lina," he said. "Go back to the National Team. Apologize to the coach. Do your pushups. Rejoin the team."

I turned and began to hit the bag.

Omar started screaming. "Here is how it will be. You will either do as I say – you will apologize and rejoin the team – or you are banned from my dojo – forever."

I picked up my bag and left.

At home, Mother and I had a long talk.

"I am so angry," I said. "I have trained harder than anyone – I am better than almost everyone. But no one will give me a chance. All they care about is the family name."

"What do you want to do?" she asked.

Empowering Women Through Self-Defense

"I'll tell you what I won't do." I saw flashbacks of Jamal – the girls in school making fun of my hair – the boys who had pushed me and teased me. "I will not apologize. I am finished with telling people I am sorry for being who I am. Coach Omar's family dominates the Federation – the head of the Federation is his uncle. I will not apologize."

Mother patted me on the head. "Follow your heart," she said. "God will tell you what to do."

Humiliation covered me again. I was forever done with the national team.

***

I was free. No more politics. No more corruption. No more, "Drop and do fifty!" from coaches who were more interested in hassling me than in training me. I could do whatever I wanted to do.

And what I wanted to do was what I had wanted to do since I was a kid…

…play soccer.

I joined a women's team and had a blast. My teammates accepted me – they were athletes; I was no longer the "weird girl who acted like a boy."

Then, it all changed.

In the middle of a tight game, I was headed down the left side. I saw two defenders converging on my position – and I saw the hole. From my vantage point, it looked as wide as a parking space. I knew I could get through, drive to the goal and score.

I accelerated, planted my leg and pushed.

I heard the crack – I felt the pain – and I blacked out.

***

"Why am I here?" I asked.

A doctor leaned in – he was in scrubs – instinctively, I braced for bad news.

"Lina," he said. "You have torn your ACL."

Chapter 5

The Long Road Back

Failure is another steppingstone to greatness.
                              Oprah Winfrey

I felt the color drain from my face. Something like a fever ran through my veins.

"Am I done as a fighter?" I asked.

"Yes, I'm sorry." His face did not carry any emotion. I wasn't the first "former" athlete he'd seen. "We have to operate. You probably have internal bleeding."

As he headed to the door, Mom entered. The doctor put his hand on her shoulder.

"After the surgery, keep ice on her knee. She can go home now. Nothing to eat or drink after midnight. We will see you tomorrow at 5:30 AM."

No one spoke on the way home. I wanted to cry, but I held everything inside. I could see Jamal's leering face – I could feel the rock hitting my eye – I remembered the warmth of wetting myself. Every humiliation of my life came flooding back to my mind.

My dreams of training and continuing as a fighter now rested in the same graveyard as my Olympic aspirations. Things got worse.

"You are done with Taekwondo," Father said. I could see his pulse throbbing through a vein in his forehead. He clenched his jaw. His nostrils flared. "I never want to hear you talk about that silly sport again. I knew this would happen."

"But I hurt my knee playing football," I said.

"Football, taekwondo, what does it matter. You should not have been doing any of those things. Why can't you be like your mother and sister and do the sorts of things women are intended to do?" He kept repeating his mantra as he stormed down the hall. "I knew this would happen."

I lay on my bed; an ice bag swaddled my knee. The ceiling never changed. I know because I stared at it for hours – all afternoon – and all evening. When the pain came, it stayed – all night.

***

You know the definition of "routine surgery"? It's something the doctor is doing to someone else. The next morning, I "crutched" my way into the hospital.

Mother was not there. In a freakish and freakishly-timed accident, she had burned her face. A cooking pot exploded the night after my accident; the contents seared her skin. Mother was not allowed out of the house – the physicians feared that exposure to the Middle Eastern sun would damage her skin beyond repair. In addition, I now had a baby sister, Reem. Mother could not leave her alone.

My friend Alia took me to the hospital.

Father refused to go to the hospital with me.

And I was terrified.

The nurses were funeral home quiet. They knew a dead athletic career when they saw one.

 Empowering Women Through Self-Defense

The only solace I took was in my faith. "God will provide," I told myself. "He will send an angel."

I was in my early twenties – not wise – and certainly not experienced. But I trusted.

"Count backwards from one hundred," the anesthetist said.

"You are trying to put me to sleep," I said. "I do not want to…"

"Well, then," "she said, "What are the names and numbers of the players on your favorite football team? Tell me. I want to know.

I was pretty goofy by this time. I don't remember getting to the second name. I vaguely remember asking, "Why am I laughing," then thick darkness surrounded me. I was never asleep, but I could not clear the veneer of black velvet from inside my head. It was the strangest thing. The next words I remember saying are, "Cold…I'm cooooold." I was in a double room. The girl next to me was Syrian. A woman (I learned it was the girl's mother) raced over and covered me with a few blankets. Then, she turned off the air conditioner.

When I awakened again, I remembered enough to be polite.

"Thank you for taking care of me," I said.

She nodded quietly.

"Is that your daughter?"

"Yes, she has food poisoning."

This Syrian mother – the face of an angel – the touch of a healer – took care of me as if I was her own. I never even knew her name. When she left (her daughter improved), I was on my own.

Father stopped by for five minutes. He gave his one-line speech. "I do not ever want to hear you talk about Taekwondo again." Then he left.

A word here. My father is a good man ... a very good man. I know he loves me, and I know he is, and has always been, proud of me. But we are all products of our upbringing. He grew up in a family of fourteen children. Poor does not accurately describe his early life.

There were too many mouths to feed – and too many people talking. Father never learned much about the art of communication – well, he learned one thing: men never talk about their feelings. It is considered a sign of weakness.

He started his business from scratch and clawed his way to success. His company manufactures chalk boards and white boards for schools and universities and exports them to the Middle East/ North Africa (MENA) region. All of his brothers work at the company. Father continues to pay the education costs for countless nieces and nephews.

He has huge and weighty responsibilities. If he doesn't always express his affection and care very well, he gets a pass from me.

He's earned it.

***

The shift nurse was rude and obviously too busy to bother.

I pushed the call button.

"What?"

"I need to use the toilet," I said.

"I can't help you. Too busy."

"But I have to go – now." I had waited as long as I could.

"You have to stay in bed. I can bring you a glass or you can pee in the bed."

Images of Math class returned along with the horror and humiliation.

A voice broke into my dilemma. "Good morning, Lina."

"Alia!" I had seldom been so happy to see someone – anyone. I attended the University with Alia.

"I hate to ask."

"What do you need?"

"Can you help me to the bathroom?"

She reached down to assist. We moved at a ridiculously slow pace, but it was all I could manage. I screamed in pain with every weight shift and every movement. When the sheet slid across the point of incision, I felt fire in my knee. The entire ordeal took approximately forever, but we got it done.

Alia stayed and fed me dinner.

First a woman who had never met me before – now, my friend from school. The realization hit me like Jamal's rock: When you are really in need, these were the emissaries from God, angels in human form.

The heaviness in my chest lessened – the negative thoughts began to break apart – I could sense the small but steady rays of emotional sunlight trying to poke past the gloom in my heart.

Stay positive, I told myself. Things will get better. They always have.

I was in my twenties. I thought I had life by the tail – that I had figured everything out. Wasn't true, of course, but I was beginning to get an idea. And I had learned a valuable lesson: Setbacks are not the same as failure. Setbacks simply require you to reroute your life a little.

Going home was good. I had not lost hope and I had learned a little something about patience.

Good thing, because I had another hill to climb.

The surgeon had made several mistakes or miscalculations. Apparently, the swelling had not subsided completely by the time I went under the knife. Subsequently, the physician could not see or repair all the damage. Depending on your perspective, the arthroscopic procedure had either been a partial success or a partial failure.

I hold to the second opinion. Even after rehab, I could not stretch properly. I continued to suffer from discomfort, particularly in my back.

I needed another operation. At the time, I was studying French. One of my classmates told me about a doctor in Lyon, France.

Empowering Women Through Self-Defense

"He is a miracle worker," she said.

I contacted her surgeon, then approached my father. To my great joy, Father agreed to bear the cost of the procedure. My mother and Reem accompanied me to France.

The hospital was small, but spotlessly clean and wonderfully efficient. A side note – even these wonderful nurses would not let me out of bed to pee. Apparently, it's a thing. I had to keep the leg elevated.

After twenty-one long days, I began therapy again – light exercise, swimming, biking   absolutely no weight work. My spirits remained high – I had faith and hope.

Retraining muscles is tough – and painful. I had no idea why things were happening, but I quit worrying about the "why." I began to focus on the "how" of recovery.

Master Ali came to see me. "You only need time," he said. "Time and faith. Do not give up. You will be stronger than before – if not on the outside, certainly on the inside. Take the time to heal. It will be fine."

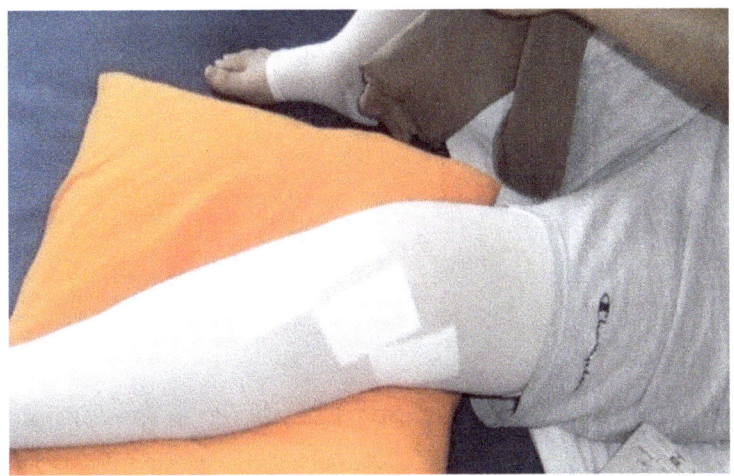
Knee Surgery

Mother was there. "Thank you for coming over," she said.

"A pleasure," he said. "By the way, did you ever get your medal." Mother looked puzzled.

"The gold medal you should have been awarded for encouraging and supporting Lina. She would never have succeeded in Taekwondo or in this recovery without your help."

I was on crutches for a while. I could not practice, of course. But I dedicated myself to recovery. Still, the leg never regained championship form.

Mom recovered from the burns on her face. Throughout her ordeal, which was both frightening and painful, she remained positive. She always believed that she will get her face beautiful back again. So, she did.

I still could not figure out the "why."

But it would become clear in the future.

Chapter 6

Sara Starts It

*Logic will get you from A to B;
Imagination will take you everywhere.*

Albert Einstein

Recovery took a little longer than I expected ... several years. My days as a competitor were gone, but I slowly worked myself back into shape. In 2004, I was in my second year and was attending a well-respected university and majoring in French Literature.

I had developed a passion for languages. I was good in communication and a fast learner – I was not as stupid as I had been led to believe. In addition to French, I learned Spanish and Italian.

Women comprised eighty percent of the French Department. Ours was a typical institute of higher learning – women stuck to "girlie" things like languages and teaching – men studied engineering and business. Although I was enjoying my studies, I had no plan for the future. After all, how many French Lit majors does the world really need?

I loved most of the aspects of university life, but there was one significantly dark area – the University was a haven for harassment. I never felt comfortable walking to lectures; I made it a point to avoid going alone. The male students constantly made loud comments about my outfit – they rushed women and tried to wrangle telephone numbers.

I didn't have any experience in situations like this. Sure, Jamal bullied me because he did not want me to play with the boys, but I had never been in a place where every woman was a target for a lewd comment, a casual shoulder rub, or a blatant advance. This was supposed to be a university not a singles' bar.

I was hurrying to a lecture one morning; I was a little late. Sara was sitting on the Library steps. I slowed my jog long enough to see that she was crying.

"What's wrong?" I asked.

She shook her head. She would not look at me and she was shielding the left side of her face with a handkerchief.

"Sara, what is wrong?"

She removed the linen. Her swollen eye reminded me of Jamal, his rock, and my bruised face.

"What happened?"

Between sniffles, she managed, "It's a family matter. Please do not interfere."

I took a napkin from my bag and began to wipe her tears. She flinched every time I got anywhere near her eye – not from pain – from fear.

"You know, my sister and I work part-time here at school to pay for our education."

I nodded.

"My brother thinks I should give the money to him," she said. "This morning, he started yelling and demanding the money. When I refused, he slapped me; then he punched me."

"Did you tell your father?"

She laughed. It was a deeply sarcastic, angry chuckle. "My father," she said, "Would only help with the beating. I am twenty-one. My sister is twenty-six. They treat us like slaves."

I couldn't think of a single, comforting thing to say. "Did you call the police."

This time, Sara burst into actual laughter. "You think they would help? They would have said, 'Be good women and listen to your father and brother.' After they left, the beating would have gotten worse."

She was right. We live in a society dominated by men. More accurately, we live in a land where women have less than no standing. I'd always believed I was free. The older I became, the more I understood my "freedom" was a very bad joke. What mattered – no, all that mattered – was protecting the rights and honor of the men and honor of the families

We hugged. "Don't worry," I said. "We will find a solution. Now, go to the toilette, wash your face, and we will go to our lectures.

"We've already missed most of the first one," she said. "Let's go get coffee before the second."

Empowering Women Through Self-Defense

She hurried away, and I sat and thought about what I had said. "We will find a solution." What in the world does that mean? I have no solution.

But I had been fighting for over ten years – this was simply a bigger fight.

I arrived at the University very early the next day and sat outside under a tree, my coffee in my hand. Things needed to change – and I had promised a solution. What did I have to offer?

Why are women victims? Do men think we are weak? Is it because we will not speak out?

Students wandered onto campus and lecture time approached. Winter was sliding into spring. The Earth was awakening from its season's-long nap. It was time for the women in Jordan to escape from the centuries'-long fear.

All the way into class, questions pounded my brain. Lina, why are you more confident than your friends?

The answer was clear: Martial Arts. My physical and mental training had sharpened by senses and my physique to a razor's edge. Other women and girls needed to feel what I felt, know what I knew, and believe in themselves with the same confidence I felt pumping through my body.

What if women were trained like me?

A voice in my head would not stop, Start today.

Empowering Women Through Self-Defense

Would they have to fight, or would their elevated self-confidence stop an attack before it stopped?

Start today.

Was it possible to remove a "victim's mindset" from an entire culture? Start today?

And, if they are, indeed, attacked, can they learn how to fight back?

"Lina?" The professor was standing right in front of me. I had not seen her. "Lina, are you paying attention?"

"Yes," I said. "Yes, I am."

I just was not paying attention to her. I was listening to the voice.

Start today!

After class, I went to the gym. I sat on the floor and stared at my reflection in the mirror. Suddenly – maybe for the first time in my life – I liked what I saw. I liked everything about me – everything I had become.

It's a good thing no one came into the gym – they might have thought I'd lost my mind because I started talking to my reflection.

"Who can do it better than you, Lina?" I asked. "Who is more passionate? Who is more qualified? You can do this – you can train women – you can teach women how to defend themselves."

I moved into a fighting stance and looked at the mirror one more time. This time I said it out loud.

"Start today!"

Chapter 7

Basement Beginnings

The secret of getting ahead is getting started.
Mark Twain

I wracked my brain. There had to be an answer.

Women for Themselves – no.

The name would not come.

Let me back up a bit. Father had given permission for me to use the basement. It was 70 square meters (+700 square feet). I have 500 Jordan dinars (approximately 700$ USD) in savings. And I wanted to start training women.

Training Women for Tomorrow – no.

In addition to preparing for the two students I had, I needed to find a way to expand my business plan. A pair of women does not make a martial arts empire!

Stay positive. It is wonderful to train girls – to train women.

Okay, what was the main focus? To end violence again women.

How was I doing to accomplish the goal? By teaching self-defense techniques.

Fighting Females – hell no!

I kept working on the business plan. I listed the name of every woman I knew and made notes about whether they might be interested.

Female … Woman … Her … Feminine … Boxers … Battlers … Defenders.

It was in there – I would find it.

Her … no – She … Wolves … oh, that is really terrible … She … Boxers … no, I am a Fighter … She-Fighters!

No … SheFighter!

I danced around the room. I had it.

***

"SheFighter, what do you think?" I looked at Alia expectantly when I told her later in the day.

"Dumbest thing I ever heard," she said. "Boring."

In truth, I was past the point of caring. I loved SheFighter – and I was going with it. In the following days, I asked more people. Alia's comment was the only negative one I ever heard.

I bought some puzzle mats, a punching bag, a kicking target, and two jump ropes. As soon as I posted my announcement on Facebook, I began to get calls. Over 700 people "liked" my announcement in the first week.

The phone calls were a mixed bag.

"Wow, this sounds great."

"What do you mean classes are in your basement?"

Offering two, one-hour classes a week, I signed a couple of students and started SheFighter. The classes grew steadily. The girls and women began to open up about their stories – harassment, sexual assaults, and domestic violence.

I started research on "targets" – what age females endure assault and harassment the most. Teens led in the both the abuse and harassment categories. I decided to begin self-defense workshops at schools and universities.

When I walked into the first school with a proposal, I was thrilled. I was offering a real opportunity for advancement and safety. The School's administrator was far less enthusiastic.

"We don't need such training – girls are not into self-defense."

Not a problem. I had expected some pushback. "Why don't you let me make a brief presentation and we can find out?"

The answer did not change. "No. You cannot speak to our female students. They are not interested in boys' sports."

When did defense become a sport? I thought.

Discouragement sank onto my shoulders as I headed for the car. Then I remembered Master Ali's advice, "There is no disgrace in losing. There is only disgrace in accepting defeat as a way of life."

Self-defense teaches a lot about reflection – how to focus inward. I took time and searched within. What was my purpose – to succeed? To prosper?

Empowering Women Through Self-Defense

No, I wanted to help people. Specifically, I wanted to help victimized women and I wanted to train women to avoid becoming victims. It's a worthy cause, Lina.

Teaching people to fight so they can hurt other people is not worthy. Teaching people to fight for a cause – for justice and equality – well, I cannot think of many higher callings.

The basement classes continued. I have not stopped teaching since. It was not always easy. Sometimes I sat in the small space and stared at the four walls. I looked into the lone mirror I had mounted so fighters could check their positioning. I stared at the single punching bag and remembered the array of equipment in Master Ali's dojo. The solitary kicking target looked alone and ludicrous.

But they were symbols – indicators of greater things.

After a while, I realized the basement would not hold more than ten. Money was scarce; I could not afford a studio. I began to contact the gyms in Amman and inquired about renting rooms. With their permission, I began a relentless marketing campaign for SheFighter.

One gym was particularly enthusiastic. They saw the "value add" of a class pinpointed to women and girls. After negotiating a price and times (twice a week for three months), I rushed to the bank. When I returned with the cash, I left some flyers on the Reception Desk.

We began the "Great Experiment" with a free workshop. Over forty women attended. I was mortified. What was I going to do to impress them – to get them to return – to pay?

Empowering Women Through Self-Defense

I have two lines I use all the time. Whether or not I used them at the first meeting, I honestly cannot recall. But I hope I did.

"If you want to make a change, quit complaining." And…

… "When life punches you in the face and throws you to the ground, stand up and say, 'You punch like a baby.'"

I introduced the SheFighter concept. I talked about the importance of women's self-defense. I emphasized I was not trying to turn anyone into an aggressor – or to make anyone less feminine. My sole desire was to help them understand the injustice and impermanent status of victimhood.

When I began the physical training, as we walked through the basics of self-defense, I felt the energy level rise. Women started smiling. The room radiated happiness.

After an amazing first day, I took to social media to advertise workshops, seminars, and classes. The numbers grew steadily. I contacted more gyms.

More gyms said yes. Maybe they did not want to be the first – but no one wanted to be last either. Soon, I was in a trio of gyms, each with an assortment of excited women and girls engaged in robust classes.

I had negotiated separate, six-month deals in each location. As I neared the completion of the first six months, one of the gym owners asked me to step into his office.

His opening stunned me. "You are providing SheFighter classes in other gyms. Stop it or you will have to leave here."

I blinked, not believing what I was hearing. "I rent space from you. What I do here is my business. I've never hidden the fact I am in other locations."

"Well," he said. "We did not anticipate the large number of people. You either continue with us exclusively, or you have to leave."

It was the National Federation all over again. And this clown received the same sort of response. "You will not have to kick me out – I am leaving. You can explain to your customers why you don't have SheFighter classes any longer."

The next day, I had a similar meeting at Gym 2#. "We cannot provide space for you any longer," the manager (a woman) said. "We need more room for open sessions."

"We have a deal in place," I said. "I have the next three months."

"Your money will be returned. We just need the space."

Things were beginning to smell a little fishy. I had a truckload of questions bombarding my brain as I walked out of the building.

Why they are kicking me out?

What did I do wrong?

Do I have too many clients?

Am I a threat?

And the biggest one.

What do I do now?

The next day, I made a preemptive strike and told the third gym I was leaving. I bet they were relieved. As I exited, I was smiling.

Chapter 8

SheFighter

The First Self-Defense Studio for Women in the Middle East

SheFighter was homeless.

I asked God to guide me – I asked every night when I went to bed.

God remained silent.

At least for a while.

Clients kept calling. "When are you going to start again? Have you found a spot?"

"You will know as soon as I do," was my constant response.

One morning, I got a different kind of call. "Lina, there is a dojo available."

"Huh?' Not my best response, but I was a little surprised.

"The owner wants to travel to the States. He is looking for someone to rent his space. There's a bathroom, a shower, a training space, and a reception area. It's not real big, but you won't lose anything by checking it out."

I called the owner while I was changing my clothes and asked to check the space. He gave me the address. When I entered the space, he was waiting for me. Even empty, I could tell it was a dojo.

We shook hands and he gave me a tour. The training space was only about 100 square meters, but I knew it would suffice. Start small and build. Sunlight poured in through large windows. I liked it.

Not wanting to show my hand, I said, "I need to check with some folks. Can I bring some people by to see the place?"

"Any time," he said.

Mother said she would look the next day. Alia said, "I can be there in an hour."

"It's great," Alia said. "How are you going to pay for it."

That very thought had been pounding in my brain for the last ninety minutes. "I'll figure it out," I said.

"Go for it, Lina," she said.

With an appointment with the owner at noon on the next day secured, I headed home. My pulse raced as I got closer to the house. I could see hundreds of women, all training, all wearing SheFighter shirts. I did not know very much about finances, but I cobbled together a budget and presented a plan to my father. He listened patiently.

"It's a nice hobby," he said. "I don't want you to get your hopes up too high because it will hurt when this fails. But, since you are so set and since you have worked so hard, I will loan you 4000 dinars (5600$ USD). You must pay me back. Do you understand?"

At that point, I would have agreed to wrestle a python. "Yes, Father," I said. "I understand."

"One suggestion," he said. "Make your memberships for a duration of three months. That way, no one can be angry when you shut down in ninety days."

It was not exactly a great pep talk.

We signed the contract the next day and I launched SheFighter in June 2012 ,2 and it became The First Self-Defense Studio for Women in the Middle East!

***

Wouldn't this be a great story if I started SheFighter and everything worked?

Might be a great story, but it would not be realistic – and it wouldn't be true. Most people struggle before success appears. SheFighter was no different.

The space issues were daunting, but I eventually solved them with a little shoe leather and some luck. Getting a license for the business presented an entirely different issue. I explained the idea to the good people in the Licensing Office. They looked at me as if I had sprouted a second head.

"Huh?"

I went through the concept again.

"So, it's a Taekwondo school."

"No," I said.

"It's a fitness gym?"

"No," I said.

5 year old girl drew Lina providing a workshop

I must have outlined the concept fifty times – every time the stare got blanker and the future looked bleaker. Finally – and I mean after a very long time – I happened across a female official who wholeheartedly supported women's rights – not the most common creature in Jordan.

I've explained the staffing issues, problems that continued to plague SheFighter. We were like a teenager, growing so fast that our shoes were always the wrong size.

But the single, greatest obstacle came in the form that inflexible monolith of tradition, culture. Trying to convince people (both male and female) that women should even be interested in self-defense was like trying to pole vault over The Eiffel Tower. Some of my best friends refused to support my idea.

Registration, branding, and licensing took about three months and I announced the opening of classes.

The 1st Self-Defense studio for women, "SheFighter," is finally open and ready to train women and girls from different age groups.

Ten students arrived in the first month, but the numbers continued to grow ... then to boom. As the months passed, my excitement gave way to exhaustion. I was operating SheFighter alone – and teaching every minute of every class.

Hiring an assistant seemed like a no-brainer. One of the students was a former boxing champion. When I offered to train her in self-defense, she jumped at the chance. At the beginning, she was dedicated and cooperative. As time wore on, her enthusiasm gave way to complaining. She didn't like her salary ... or her hours ... or – well – anything.

I begged for patience. "We are only starting," I said.

The carping continued.

After a while, I could not take the energy drain any longer – I let her go.

I hired another – then another – then another. None of them lasted.

Why doesn't anyone want to work with me? I thought. I considered the issue from every possible angle and finally hit on a solution.

Build a team – how hard can that be?

As it turns out – very – very hard.

I continued working, closing the gym every night at 9 PM after a full day of classes. The dream was coming together – and killing me – all at the same time. I had to create a system.

Why not train the trainers yourself? The idea was so simple, I kicked myself for not considering it before. If I took my trainers from start to finish, I could choose the best as my assistants.

I began the manual the next day. With no experience in writing and very little talent in drawing, putting together the "how-to" with illustrations proved challenging. But I have always loved a good challenge. I kept sketching the techniques until each one was just right.

SheFighter combines different disciplines. We have competitions, but they are very controlled and internal. I do not want anyone injured. We compete solely for training – and for a little fun. I combined elements of taekwondo, kung fu, boxing, and Aikido for self-defense like choke holds and hair grabs. The concept tailors itself to a woman's unique physique and (occasional) physical limitations.

The hardest part about the writing was – the writing. I made myself start. Once I began, the words started flowing out of the pen like they had a mind of their own. After a few months, I had my "Level System."

There are five:

1) The Pink Level/ Beginner

To be certified on the Pink Level, trainers must finish 22 hours of training, then they need to pass a test (passing grade of 75) and completing 8 hours of shadowing. Shadowing means that each potential SheFighter trainer follows a higher-level trainer during classes – observing and making notes. They assist the instructor in teaching the techniques.

2) The Silver Level/ Intermediate

22 hours of intensive training, a test, and another 4 hours of shadowing.

3) The Black Level/ Advanced

Another 22 hours of training (you did not think it would get easier, did you?), a test, and 4 more shadowing hours. Instructors at higher levels are more experienced. They "get" the moves faster, so they have more time to perfect them.

4) The Gold Level/ Professional

When you complete this stage, you will have had 84 hours of training (another 22 for Gold Level).

Empowering Women Through Self-Defense

5) The Master Level/ Masters

This is the highest level in the SheFighter system. When you complete this stage, you will have 110 hours of training – there are 26 more hours required for this level) and you are a "Master." That's the higher and last level at SheFighter system. You become officially Master at SheFighter when passing the Master Level.

The tests have 5 components: technique test, managing target test, self-defense techniques, fight competition (this is a "light fight" with full protective gear), and coaching skills (primarily theory). The "managing" test needs some explanation. It involves learning to hold training (focus) mitts properly – if they are not positioned correctly, fighters can suffer injury. Two Master level trainers administer the test. One watches the candidate and gives the instructions; the other assesses and gives the marks. I train and test all Masters.

Once again, I turned to social media – this time to promote the "TOT" (Training of Trainers) course. I highlighted that the women who were interested only needed passion for the concept, not expertise in the field. On the second day, I started getting phone calls. Most of the ones (at least at the beginning) who were interested were already my students.

By the time I had worked my classes through the Pink Level, I had four women interested in becoming certified SheFighter Trainers. I was not sure if I was on the right track. But the more I trained others, the less nervous I was. I saw the delight ... the skill ... and the confidence growing in every student.

***

My struggles were not over. In general, people resist change – society tends to fight against it. Middle Eastern society and change – not a happy combination.

People began to toss nails in my path. Jordan (like the other countries in the region) has ways to deal with conflict – unofficially assigned by gender. Women combat discord by talking ugly about those involved – "Well, you know, she…"

Middle Eastern men rush to tradition, then to the legal system. At first, "We have always done things this way." Or –when dealing with the females in the family – "Women are supposed to…" Outside the family, every disagreement devolves into a lawsuit or a police report.

Suzan was a student and a very bright woman and, uh oh, a feminist. She had earned a master's degree in Women's Studies. After she studied with me for a year, she became engaged to a lawyer – apparently, not a very good one. He was failing in his profession. Things did not improve for him on the career front after the wedding, which he must have blamed either on Suzan or on me – she quit coming to SheFighter classes.

Like any decent teacher, I contacted her.

"I cannot come," she said. "I am busy."

A week later, I was informed that her husband had instituted a lawsuit against my business because SheFighter had taught his wife how to beat him up. There is a law in Jordan – if anyone tries to ruin a marriage, they can be sentenced to jail from three months to three years.

Although I did not have a lot of money, I knew my future was on the line, so I hired an attorney. We tried to solve the issue amicably. The husband was insistent.

"I don't want Suzan to go to your classes anymore. You are interfering with my life and our marriage."

It was a monstrous lie, but Jordanian law was on his side. Once Suzan pledged never to return to SheFighter, he dropped the legal action.

***

I cannot count how many times men came to my studio to threaten me or my students.

One of my trainers had a brother who was a particular problem. Somehow, he got my cell phone number. He kept calling.

"Make my sister quit. She should not be working in that place."

That place – he made it sound like we were doing something illegal or immoral. We were helping people.

"I cannot make her quit," I said. "It is her decision because (and I emphasized the next part) it is her life!"

Apparently, he disagreed. He showed up at the studio where he and his sister had a savage verbal argument. I let it go – their concern and no one was being violent – until he said the magic words, "You will do what I say, or I will kill you."

I called the police. He ran away – once again, Jamal the coward fleeing the scene before he can be punished by someone in authority.

***

SheFighter attracts women from every walk of life – and from every station. Another of my trainers was the daughter of a man with considerable influence in Jordan – he occupied a lofty position.

"Fire my daughter," he said.

"I'll talk to her," I said. I had no intention of letting her go. She was one of my best employees and an accomplished trainer. Her father's inability to handle the situation was his problem.

"I am sorry my father is bothering you," she said. "Please, do not listen to him. I love it here and I want to stay."

I assured her I was not going to dismiss her – certainly not because of her father.

She quit a little later. The pressure from her family was too great.

The pressure on me was tremendous and I could feel my focus slipping away from my mission to help women. I realized what I was enduring was just part of the empowerment journey. "Lina, it will be fine. Push through. Keep your eye on the prize."

The pep talk (to myself) worked!

***

Almost without exception, the neighbors around the dojo hated SheFighter. The concept confused and annoyed them. When I opened in the morning, I heard, "You should not be doing this." At night as I turned the key in the lock, someone would invariably shout, "Stop teaching our wives to hit us." Many were annoyed by concept. They Would all call me names. "You are the woman teaching our wives how to beat us up."

These were not "punks" or drifters; these were businessmen. One man continually pulled his car right behind mine, blocking me. Every time I asked him to move – politely – he yelled at me, called me hateful names, and told me how much he disapproved of my work.

"I have been here much longer than you," he said. "You should not even park here."

He kept blocking my car even after I asked him, very politely, to stop. In truth, I do not remember the resolution, but I do recall I had to make police reports about harassment at least a half dozen times.

***

It wears on you after a while – the hatred – the distrust – the suspicion – the opposition – other people's fear. I tried to stay positive and I succeeded, mostly. Some days, however, when I awakened, my first thought was Why do I have to deal with pettiness?

I never let anyone stop me. Even when the police refused to help, I went back and asked for help again. After a while, they knew I was serious – and that I was not going to stop.

There were some funny things, at least in an ironic way. One man kept yelling at my students. He threatened them. He called to them. "You should not be here – you cannot park there." What was funny? Well – a year later, his daughter signed up for classes.

Men tried to break down my door. Fortunately, I had security cameras and could prove my claim when I called the authorities. I cannot think of a single name I have not been called – and Jordanian men can be quite creative when they wish to be vile. I've been threatened with legal action, arrest, and violence.

Focus slipped away sometimes – discouragement laid a hand across my shoulder and whispered, "Don't you think it's time to quit?" The continual negativity drained me to the point of absolute fatigue.

Photo credited to Marta Malas

But every time I saw a new student – hesitant and unsure – every time I stood in front of a class – every time someone told me they had stood up for themselves or staved off an attack, my energy and resolve returned.

SheFighter is not about me – it never was.

Photo credited to The Atlas of beauty

Chapter 9

What It Takes

*The greatest love of all is easy to achieve.
Learning to love yourself is
the greatest love of all.*

Linda Creed/Michael Masser

Would it surprise you if I were bitter? After all, I have been battling as long as I can remember. Starting with Jamal – the mean girls in my school – an insensitive math teacher – crooked Federation officials – a bureaucracy stacked against female business owners – rampant opposition from an ancient, inflexible, male-dominated culture.

Would you blame me if I remained angry?

Maybe not, but I would be disappointed in myself. In truth, I am happy and content – and I have been for a long time because I have remained true to myself, my goals, and my vision.

Back when it all started, the basement of my house never grew. Concrete walls do not miraculously move (like something out of Harry Potter) just because we want more room. It was 2013 and 2014. SheFighter was not a reality – it was not even a thought. I was just an individual teaching self-defense in a concrete basement.

But in my mind, the space (both physical and mental) continued to expand. I began to see the future. Whenever I sat in the basement planning SheFighter, whenever I had a class – whether there were ten students or only one – whenever I worked out in front of the mirror, checking my positions, ensuring my technique was good enough to teach to others – I could see something new … sometime exciting … something different.

And by the time I had the name and a clearer idea of what I wanted to accomplish; I knew SheFighter would work.

I loved it when people told me I was crazy. Their pessimism drove me.

Many times, I visualized the future. I saw what SheFighter could become – what it would become

Whenever you add people to your life or to your organization, you add personalities and opinions. Everyone has a different outlook. And that can be good – diverse approaches can lead to success. Listening to someone else's suggestion often leads to meaningful and impactful change.

At SheFighter, we love diverse opinions – but we do not tolerate diverse attitudes. What you believe is your business but stay positive.

Sometimes, finances teetered on the brink of "scary." I never let myself panic. I made sure I was informed – you have to be realistic – but I never let myself be unnerved. I knew we had a good plan … a good mission … a great purpose. I always believed SheFighter would make it.

Every so often, we would attract a diva – someone with great skills (maybe better than mine) – a great martial artist. But she emitted negative energy because it was all about her. She had to leave. Remember, "one bad apple spoils the entire barrel."

Again, SheFighter is not interested in robots. Everyone does not have to agree on everything. But we remain upbeat and focused on improvement.

Somewhere early on, I realized the journey was not about changing women's lives. Well, not the entire journey. Helping other women (and girls and boys – I reach out to help young men) represents a happy, helpful byproduct. But the journey is mine – my quest for meaning – my trip to self-discovery.

I am still traveling the road – still learning things – and always loving the voyage.

I was the outcast – the girl with bad hair – the miserable math student – the ugly kid in the class. As I mentioned in the first chapter, I did not fit in with everyone else – I didn't fit with anyone. The girls thought I was weird – the boys, well, they knew I was a girl, so they did not want me around.

My father was confused by me – I think my mother might have been a little afraid for me.

Life is about learning – about uncovering what lies inside – underneath the skin – the things living, sometimes hiding, in your heart. And I started my trek in the basement.

I am a big fan of Rumi (thirteenth century Persian poet and Islamic scholar). This passage continually speaks to me:

Two Kinds of Intelligence

> There are two kinds of intelligence: one acquired, as a child in school memorizes facts and concepts from books and from what the teacher says, collecting information from the traditional sciences as well as from the new sciences.
>
> With such intelligence you rise in the world. You get ranked ahead or behind others in regard to your competence in retaining information. You stroll with this intelligence in and out of fields of knowledge, getting always more marks on your preserving tablets.
>
> There is another kind of tablet, one already completed and preserved inside you. A spring overflowing its spring box. A freshness in the center of the chest. This other intelligence does not turn yellow or stagnate. It's fluid, and it doesn't move from outside to inside through conduits of plumbing-learning.
>
> This second knowing is a fountainhead from within you, moving out.

Get to know yourself. Come to terms with who you are – whoever that may be. Find inner peace and life will be great. Happiness does not come from success. It's the other way around. Success flows from your own happiness.

Some people like to say, "I will fake it until I make it." Well, you cannot fake it – not for long. You might fool others for a while – maybe for a long time – but you cannot fool the Universe and you cannot fool God.

It takes a long time to come to terms with yourself. Your mind would love to take control – to convince you of things, issues, fears, and limitations that are not true. Discipline your mind, so it will follow your visions and your dreams.

My struggles with the Federation took a lot out of me. The constant conflict drained my reserves and ruined my focus. It took a while, but I have come to understand that my knee injury was a message from God: Quit spending your time and wasting your reserves on trivial political battles. Find something important. Point your life in a direction designed to make a difference. Quit arguing – start contributing.

Once you are true to yourself – life responds with boundless generosity.

Yes, there are external components. Taekwondo taught me discipline, self-control, and confidence. It helped me build singlemindedness.

Discipline … self-control … confidence … self-love … and an unshakeable positive approach … these things have led me to the point where I can help others. And those things will lead you as well.

Chapter 10

Changing Lives- One at a Time

*As I got attacked inside the elevator,
I felt I will die and couldn't breathe.*

Lubna

Tarana Burke is credited with saying, "So many people who deal with sexual harassment don›t have the means to file lawsuits or to get legal representation or legal advice." Sad, but true. And, I wanted to help the ones to whom she was referring. Little did I know I was starting a revolution.

Photo Credit to Marta Malas

When I answered the phone, I knew something was wrong.

"This is Lubna." The voice at the other end squeaked – about half an octave higher than usual – and quavered.

"Lubna, what's wrong?"

She said something. It sounded like "Gurble dinky wanda."

"Slow down. I cannot understand anything. Take your time. Everything will be fine. Breathe."

She paused. I could hear her gathering herself.

""I was attacked," she said.

"Are you okay? Do you need medical attention?"

She was obviously hanging on by a thread, but she was determined not to crack. "I am fine," she said.

"Tell me," I said. "Who was it?"

"A stranger," she said. "Never saw him before in my life. And I have absolutely no idea why. I didn't talk to him or anything."

My mind raced, flicking back across time – to all the other similar stories I knew all too well – women and girls, minding their own business, set upon by men who saw a solitary female as a "target of opportunity."

"Start at the beginning." I was aware my voice was shaking as much as hers.

"I go to work every day at 8 AM – I get home about six in the evening. Last night, I was busy – a little distracted. I didn't check around my car when I got home. I wasn't paying attention to my surroundings. I walked into my building and pressed the elevator button. I was tired and not focused. He must have sneaked up from behind me.

"When the doors slid open, a man put his hand over my mouth and pushed me inside the car. He held me against the wall. I couldn't move – I couldn't scream – I could barely breathe. He told me not to move and began to unzip my pants. I started pushing and hitting."

"You need to go the hospital," I said. "You have to make sure you are okay."

She began to laugh – not hysterically or out of control. It was a throaty laugh of triumph.

"Lina," she said when she caught her breath, "He's the one who needs to go to the hospital – wherever he is. I hit him so many times I lost count. As soon as the elevator doors opened, he took off. I chased him."

I gasped. "Oh no," I said. "You did not!"

"Yes," she said. "I was screaming like a maniac, telling him to come back, telling him I was going to beat him until he could not walk. He was terrified."

I joined in the laughter.

"He ran into the streets. I was pointing and yelling. Some other men in the street wrestled him to the ground and beat him until he blacked out."

I was speechless.

"Lina," she said. "Lina!"

"Yes, I am here."

"It's all because of you. I didn't call to report an attack. I wanted to tell you about a success, and I wanted to say thank you. I would have been a helpless victim if not for you or SheFighter."

After we said goodbye, I stared at the phone for a long time – and I knew. I was on the right track.

***

Maria had been training with SheFighter for about a year. She was in Amman from Spain – her native land. On her way home one evening, she could tell someone was following her. Panic constricted her throat. She fought for control – as she had been trained.

When the hand gripped her shoulder, she whirled and assumed the fighting stance she'd practiced for twelve months.

"He just ran away," she told me. "All I did was look like I knew what I was doing, and he fled! I think he was shocked to see a woman stand up for herself."

***

A mother brought her -26year-old daughter to us. Jana was in shock; she'd been sexually assaulted by a taxi driver. It took her a while to begin interacting, but she eventually began to "go with the flow" and interact. One afternoon – she'd been with SheFighter for about a year – she rushed into the dojo.

"A man chased me today," she said. I ran for a while, but I decided I was not going to be afraid anymore. I turned around and told him, "If you don't leave me alone, I am going to punch you in the face."

"What happened?" I asked. I was looking down at her hands for telltale bruises.

A smile broke across Jana's face. "He left!"

A few weeks later, she took me aside after class. "I rode in a taxi today," she said. "I was not scared at all."

"That's great," I said.

"And, I have decided to apply for my driving license."

Perhaps that last thing doesn't seem like a very big deal, but it is for the average woman in Jordan. For a young woman who has lived through the horror of sexual assault, taking the step that will undoubtedly lead – at some point – to being alone in a car at night … well … that is enormous.

And brave.

Photo Credit to Marta Malas

SheFighter Seminar in Kuwait

Jana was with us for two years when she decided to enroll in the TOT Program. Now she uses her background, her story, and her considerable skills to train other young women who are searching for confidence and safety.

***

One of our youngest students, a bright young girl named Mona, was eight when she started. She was tired of a culture of masculine bullying – of little boys showing off by picking on little girls – telling them, "You are stupid and weak."

She worked hard. She was not interested in hurting anyone. Despite what some of our detractors claim, she had not come to SheFighter to learn to beat up anyone.

But, one day, yet another "little tough guy" decided to demonstrate his youthful masculinity. He shoved Mona. She coiled into the fighting stance all my students know so very well.

"If you try to push me again, I will make you stop," she said.

No boy ever bothered her again.

All she said was, "Thank you for changing my life."

***

SheFighter trains the body, but it also trains the mind, often dragging it from dark and scary places into the light of hope. Samira's story is indicative of so many others.

"I hated my life. For as long as I can remember, I have been told I was not as good – not as special – not as useful. I have thought about suicide more times than I can count."

She started working with me in the training program. By the time she achieved Silver Level, her attitude had changed remarkably.

"I feel different," she said. "I have a purpose – to empower other girls. I will not go back to where I was."

SheFighter Trainers in South Korea

She served as a teacher in a local school. With the Administration's approval, she took the SheFighter system into her school where she continues to influence and embolden young women.

***

SheFighter is not about violence. We teach the opposite of brutality. We teach control – of the mind, the spirit, and the body. We are all God's creatures.

We are all worthy of respect.

We all have a right to safety.

We should all get a chance to live as we would like – in peace.

Sometimes, we must defend ourselves to protect what God wants us to have.

SheFighter – a concept whose time has come.

Chapter 11

Helping the Helpless

It is hardly possible to build anything if frustration, bitterness and a mood of helplessness prevail.

Lech Walesa

We began working with refugees when they moved to Amman. Various NGO's reached out and asked for help. The conditions were appalling and frightening. Many of the women and girls suffered sexual abuse, many times from their own relatives. Women would sell their twelve-year-old daughters as wives to Jordanian men.

I told one woman, "You cannot do that. This is not a livestock market; this is your daughter."

"We are poor. We have nothing. We have to eat," was her response.

All I could tell her was what I believe. "Have patience,

I said. "God will have mercy on you if you wait. Besides, look at all the people who are trying to help you."

I knew I could not change an entire culture, but I was (and still am) determined to do everything in my power to promote positive change. Sometimes a lawyer will remind the women that selling girls into a child marriage is illegal in Jordan, but the warning seldom stops the activity for very long.

Training and empowering orphans

We teach self-defense, how to take care of yourself when someone assaults you. But SheFighter does more. We psychologically empower women and girls, helping them to understand their self-worth – assisting them in their quest for wholeness and hope. If you want to stand up for yourself, all the Taekwondo or Aikido in the world will not do anything unless you believe you are worthy of what life can offer.

During the seminars, we try to ensure the teenaged girls will be in a position to talk with us when they are away from their mothers and grandmothers. The youngsters tend to "toe the line" when they are around an adult. Once we get "Mother" and "Grandmother" in another room, the girls are more open and honest about their needs and fears.

In 2018, I suggested utilizing refugees as trainers. We started training six Syrian women at the Pink Level. They were thrilled to have the opportunity and showed great dedication to their training. They never missed a session and passed every test with very high marks.

Women with Disabilities Training

We have a hybrid business model – a profit side and a non-profit side. We partner with non-government organizations (NGOs) to train and empower women who cannot afford to take classes – women with disabilities, orphans, women battling cancer, Syrian refugees. Every last one of them needs protection(and to build a sense of self-worth and confidence) because, as sick as it sounds, every last one of them is an easy target. Prominent NGO's in Jordan provide funding for SheFighter, which enables us to go into refugee camps and help women and girls who are vulnerable.

We continue to be blessed in our efforts to make people (especially women) safe. I was amazed the first time I visited a refugee camp. I thought I would meet terrified, meek, weak women. To my surprise, the women in the camps number among the strongest people I have ever encountered.

***

During a break in a presentation, a Syrian woman approached.

"Can we speak privately?" she asked.

We went outside. "I want to share my story with you," she said, "But I do not want you to share my name or identity."

"Of course."

"I was raped here in Jordan," she said. "A taxi driver stopped the cab and three other men jumped in. I screamed and fought, but they slapped me – they overpowered me. I kept trying to get away, but I was trapped. They raped me and threw me into the street."

Sometimes the best response is silence.

She continued. "I want the women in there to hear my story. I want them to know how important it is to learn what you are teaching. I do not want my daughters to suffer the same fate. Can you tell them that? Can you tell everyone that?"

I nodded. "Thank you for your courage," I said.

We hugged and went inside.

I did as she had asked.

***

They face life-threatening hardships every day with unflagging determination to find a better life for themselves and their families. Despite the hellish situations they continue to endure, they are positive about life and they enjoy every minute of training.

Another Syrian woman told me she watched as a little girl was kidnapped. A man snatched the child, shoved her into a minivan, and drove away. She could not forget the screams.

"Why did you not help her?" I asked in my naivete.

"He would have come back the next day for my family. But I hear that little girl's cries every night in my sleep."

"Next time, you will do something," I said.

She looked me right in the eye. "Yes, now I know I can.

Chapter 12

Its not about the Awards ..
But They are Really Nice

Keep your dreams alive. Understand to achieve anything requires faith and belief in yourself, vision, hard work, determination, and dedication. Remember, all things are possible for those who believe.

Gail Devers, Olympic Champion

The phone call fulfilled my lifelong dream. The International Olympic Committee wanted me in PyeongChang! No, I would not compete – those days were long behind me. The champion's platform was not in my future. But what I did meant far more to me than another shiny medal.

*Lina holding the torch – PyeongChang Winter Games, **2018***

I went to South Korea in 2018 and ran through the streets. My heart overflowed with happiness ... joy ... and contentment. As I ran, everyone looked – and everyone cheered. Most of them had no idea who I was.

But every last one of the spectators recognized the symbols I held as I jogged – the Olympic torch.

I was at least a decade late – but I had made it to the Olympics.

I've had other awards. In 2014, I was named as a finalist for the UNCTAD Empretec Women in Business Award. The first list contained one hundred names. After a while, the Committee cut the list to ten – then to one. The only name left was mine.

I accepted the award in Geneva at the United Nations Conference on Trade and Development in October. While I am sure I stammered during my acceptance, I was quoted as saying, "Allowing more women to learn about self-defense is my personal goal and the prize was an eye opener in this sense.»

Both the UNCTAD and the World Intellectual Property Organization supported me in obtaining global registration of the SheFighter brand internationally. Doors opened all over the world and I was invited for speaking engagements in Germany, Sweden, Holland, Italy – actually all over Europe.

Lina in Prague, Czech Republic

Empowering Women Through Self-Defense

While taking part in the Naseba's Global Women in Leadership (WIL) Economic Forum in 2016 (I was named Female Entrepreneur of the Year), I sat for an interview with Tariq Qureishy, Founder and CEO of Mad Talks. (MAD stands for "Make a Difference.")

Here are bits and pieces.

> Tariq: How big is the epidemic of the domestic violence in our part of the world?
>
> Lina: ... In the Middle East specifically, I found there is a high rate of domestic violence and the women ... do not always ... report ... for them it is getting into trouble, but it is not. It is standing up for what they believe ...
>
> Tariq: What are you fighting? Why can't we just talk about peace?
>
> Lina: I believe "fighting" is a very strong word. It has a big effect on people ... a women's journey is all about fighting – fighting to get the kids to school ... fighting since the day she is born ... it empowers her ... when I picked the name, I wanted it to be a catchy name she would never forget ... it has to be a simple name, so no one will forget it.
>
> Tariq: I'm going to press some more ... Why are we fighting? I don't want to fight. I want peace.

Lina... Unfortunately, that is life. You find negative and positive ... you find challenges and success ... violence is there; we can't deny that ... the word "fighter" is more positive than negative ... to show women that they can do this ... they are going to face obstacles.

Tariq: How does it make you feel (when someone tells you that you changed their life)?

Lina: It makes me feel amazing – like I have to keep doing what I am doing.

Awards started to pile up. They reminded me of the trophies I won as a young competitor, except every one of these meant something extra in terms of lives changed and futures altered.

***

It's easy to get lost in your own "mental trash" even when things are going well. In 2016, I was invited to Ottawa, Canada to speak at the One Young World Summit. A while before the meeting, I was sitting in a café with my laptop and working on SheFighter. I started thinking bout all the things I'd lost in the process of building my dream.

Some of my friends could not handle the success I enjoyed – or the personal growth I experiences. They were gone. I was alone – a lot – in truth, most of the time. It seemed the more I accomplished; the less people wanted to be around me. Some folks aren't comfortable with a person who can create her own path, particularly if they feel out of control in their own lives. Others find my positive mindset off-putting.

Whatever the reason, I was enjoying a cup of tea and a pity party. Then the phone rang.

"Lina, this is Phil." (He was my contact with the Ottawa Summit.)

"Good morning," I said. My mind – down in the dumps as it was at the moment – secretly feared I was being canceled.

"Are you ready for the Summit?"

Relief swept through my body. "Absolutely," I said.

"In addition to the other stuff we discussed, you are going to be part of a panel discussion on gender equity and women's rights."

"That's okay," I said. "I'm going to be there. Might as well have a complete experience. It's better than sitting around with nothing to do. What can you tell me?"

"You will be on a panel with six other people," he said.

"Great." I said."

We talked a little more. Then, I had a thought. "Why was I selected for the panel?"

"The person headlining the panel asked for you by name," he said.

"Oh," I said. "Who is that?"

He paused – now I know he paused for effect. He wanted a little drama.

"Emma Watson," he said.

Ta da!

"Seriously?"

"Absolutely. She hand-picked the panel."

Suddenly, any loss I might have been feeling was burned away by the blazing light of a revelation. This was from God – there is no other explanation. The call – the invitation – was God's way of telling me to stay focused on my blessings.

I am sure the other patrons in the café wondered what was wrong with the woman on the cell phone who was jumping up and down at her table. But I did not care.

A month later, Ms. Watson's assistant called.

"Well, Lina," she said. "You have to know that Emma really likes you and what you are doing. We all do."

"Thank you," I said.

"She has a small favor."

A little voice in my head said, "Emma Watson wants my autograph."

"Certainly," I said.

"She wonders if you could make the time to train with her for an hour at her hotel."

" Lina training Emma Watson

I almost shouted, but I stayed cool – at least on the outside. "Sure," I said. Inside, I was screaming, I am going to train Hermione Granger!"

"Please get to the hotel (she told me which one) at 8 AM the morning of the panel discussion. I will meet you in the lobby and walk you up."

The night before the meeting, I barely slept.

I was on time – I was probably an hour early, but who cares?

The assistant showed at exactly 8 AM.

"Let's go find the room we have reserved," she said.

A photographer was already set up when we arrived. A few minutes later, Emma walked in wearing leggings, training shoes, and a tank top.

"Nice to meet you," I said. "I'm Lina. This is a pleasure."

She was very nice to say, "It's a pleasure for me, too."

We warmed up a little. Things were a little awkward. I always try to keep situations like this (you know, when I meet big movie stars) casual, so I was making silly jokes. She smiled politely.

Empowering Women Through Self-Defense

Once we got into it – once we relaxed – she laughed and joked in return. She is an amazingly humble young woman. And she sounded just like she did in the movies!

Duh!

It was a great day.

***

A year later, Vital Voices informed me I had been nominated for an award at John Kennedy Center in D.C.

I could hear the blood rushing through my ears. Getting awards is exciting, but I could hear clearly enough to make out the last thing the caller said. "Hillary Clinton might be there."

In April 2018, I traveled to America again and was awarded the Vital Voices Economic Empowerment Award. Ms. Clinton was the keynote speaker.

She mentioned me!

> Tonight's honorees are proof of what can happen when inspiration meets determination. Take Lina Khalifeh, a fighter from Amman, who is giving women the strength to defend themselves from domestic violence and assault.

That evening, I delivered one of the best speeches of my life, complete with a demonstration of what I spend my life teaching.

https://www.youtube.com/watch?v=wVww4pkvbVw

Empowering Women Through Self-Defense

Photo credit to Vital Voices

Who am I? I thought. How in the world does anyone know about my work? And why am I breathing the same air as all these important people? Is this my "fifteen minutes of fame, or am I destined for something great?

I still don't know the answer to those questions, but I don't engage in self-pity anymore. I know I am on the right track – the path God has selected – and if the doors keep opening, I am going to walk through them without hesitation.

All the recognition is special. But one instance filled me with more pride than racing through the streets of PyeongChang.

Only one …

Chapter 13

"Don't Pinch Me – I Might Wake Up"

*Do not worry when you are not recognized,
but strive to be worthy of recognition.*

Abraham Lincoln

"Welcome to the White House."

Never in my wildest dreams had I imagined I would hear those words directed to me – especially not from one of the most distinguished and eloquent individuals of my lifetime – President Barack Obama. It was a White House Entrepreneurs' Event and the President was opening the festivities.

President Barack Obama

He went on for a very short time about the outstanding collection of "brain power ... innovators ... investors ... business leaders..." assembled. He spoke with his characteristic smooth, sincere intensity. Mesmerizing. I was seated among some of the guests, paying attention and minding my own business. Then, Mr. Obama almost brought me out of my seat:

> ...and we want to empower leaders of social change...like Lina...ah...Khalefah [I'm pretty sure he mispronounced my name, but did it really matter] of Jordan, where is she...there she is ... [then He – the President of the United Stated – pointed at me]. After seeing one of her close friends abused, Lina said, "That's enough," she had a background in martial arts, so she opened SheFighter, a self-defense studio for women. So far, she has helped about ten thousand women learn how to protect themselves. And now she's competing for funds to expand her mission across the Middle East. So, thank you, Lina – we want to be your partner – helping women to live with dignity and in safety.

There had been times when I doubted myself – when I wondered if I was on the right track – when I questioned whether I had what it takes to make SheFighter a viable reality. Every question … every doubt … every second guess … every uncertainty evaporated the second the Presidential Index Finger jabbed in my direction.

We had enjoyed local and regional interviews. SheFighter had appeared in newspapers, magazines, and online. When I won a few awards, I celebrated them with gusto, but hearing my name escape the lips of the most influential human being on the planet changed everything.

I had always wanted SheFighter to grow and to expand. Since the earliest days, I'd considered trying to "go global." Having visited and conducted seminars in over twenty-seven countries, I thought we had a chance. But, at that exact moment, I knew – absolutely without a smidgen of a doubt, knew – we were on the right track. I grinned so broadly, I am amazed my face did not crack. And, I smiled for days!

https://www.youtube.com/watch?v=ru8MoRS1xWY

The time Mr. Obama dedicated to me in his speech was less than a minute, but it was the most important sixty seconds of my life. As I sat in my seat, I became increasingly aware of the applause and the nodding heads. In my mind, I saw Big Bully running away and fading into the deep recesses of insignificance. Chasing behind him were thousands of women – strong, empowered women.

All of them were wearing tee-shirts emblazoned with one word: *SheFighter!*

*Lina during her Interview with **NBC**, NewYork City*

*Lina at the White House in **2015***

Empowering Women Through Self-Defense

Acknowledgements

I want to express my deep appreciation to the SheFighter Team in Amman who worked with me in building an empire of empowered women in Jordan.

Thank you to all the people who continue to support the SheFighter mission globally and who believe in the importance of Self-Defense for women

I would like to Thank my editor, Mr. Arthur Fogartie, who worked with me on this book.

I would Like to Thank My designer Rami Khalifeh who made this book an art piece.

Biography

Lina Khalifeh is the Founder and owner of SheFighter (The First Self-Defense studio for women only in Jordan and the Middle East).

SheFighter is designed to empower women physically, mentally and emotionally through Self-Defense training.

The studio has been founded in 2012 and has trained more than 18 thousand women all over the globe.

Lina has many great achievements. Some are as follows:

- President Barack Obama mentioned her in his speech at the White house in 2015.

- Lina was awarded the Stuart Scott Humanitarian ENSPIRE award presented by ESPN and UFC 2019 in Los Angeles, California.

- She was awarded "The economic empowerment Leadership" award by Hillary Clinton and Vital Voices in Washington D.C. in 2018.

- She spoke at the World Economic Forum 2019 in Davos.

Lina is very passionate about her work and is working to spread SheFighter globally and make it at reach for all women.

Check the website for more information: www.shefighter.com

www.ingramcontent.com/pod-product-compliance
Lightning Source LLC
Chambersburg PA
CBHW062034120526
44592CB00036B/2091